WELCOME TO SRI LANKA

COUNTRIES OF THE WORLD

Sri Lanka

by Kevin Kurtz

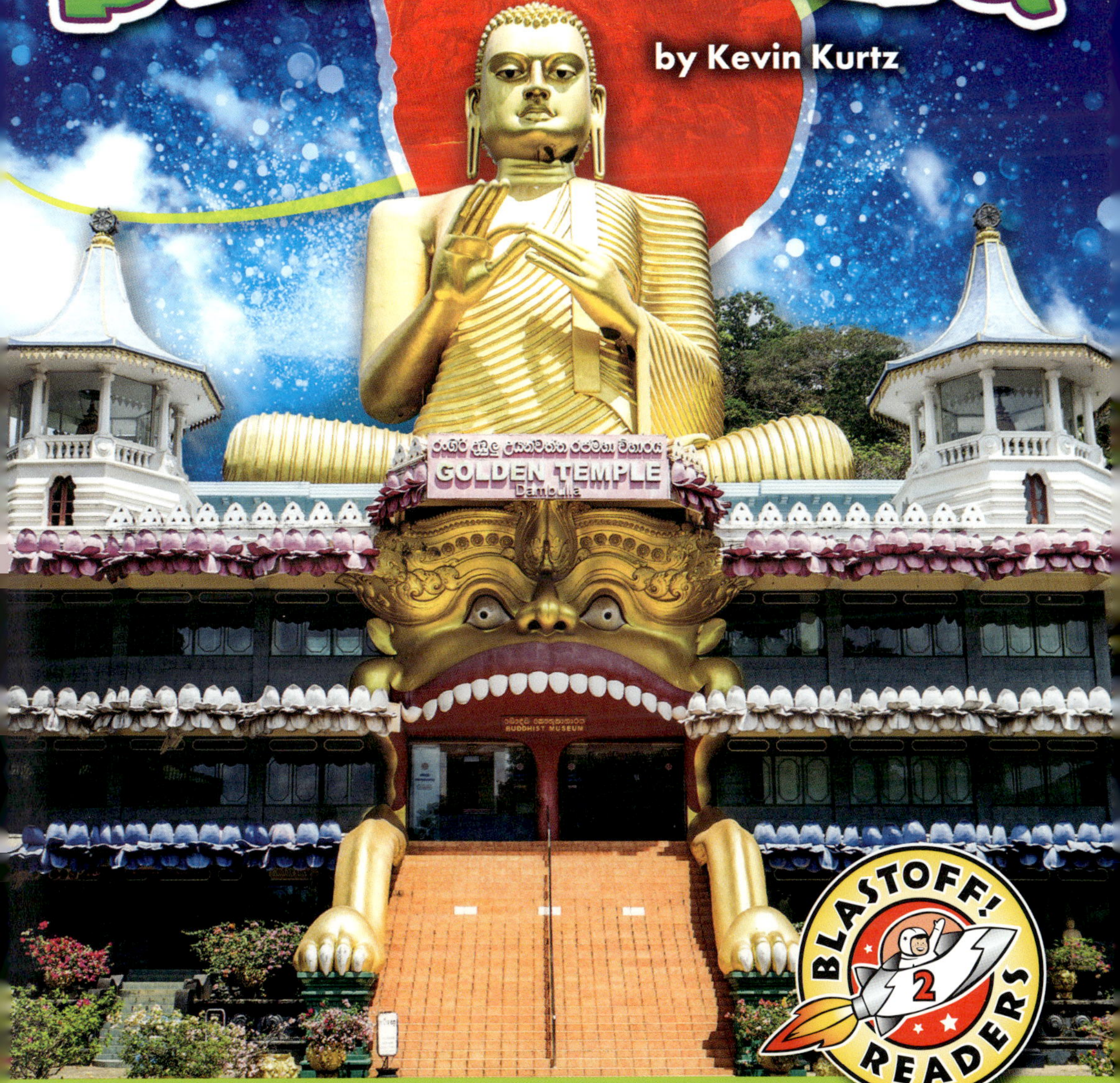

BLASTOFF! 2 READERS

BLASTOFF! READERS, AN IMPRINT OF BELLWETHER MEDIA BY FLUTTERBEE

Blastoff! Readers are carefully developed by literacy experts to build reading stamina and move students toward fluency by combining standards-based content with developmentally appropriate text.

LEVELS

Level 1 provides the most support through repetition of high-frequency words, light text, predictable sentence patterns, and strong visual support.

Level 2 offers early readers a bit more challenge through varied sentences, increased text load, and text-supportive special features.

Level 3 advances early-fluent readers toward fluency through increased text load, less reliance on photos, advancing concepts, longer sentences, and more complex special features.

★ **Blastoff! Universe**

Reading Level

Blastoff! Beginners — Grade K → Blastoff! Readers — Grades 1–3 → Blastoff! Discovery — Grade 4

This edition first published in 2027 by Bellwether Media, Inc.

For information regarding permission, write to Bellwether Media, Inc., Attention: Permissions Department, 3500 American Blvd W, Suite 150, Bloomington, MN 55431.

Library of Congress Cataloging-in-Publication Data is available at www.loc.gov or upon request from the publisher.

ISBN: 9798898800499 (hardcover)
ISBN: 9798898801731 (ebook)

Editor: Betsy Rathburn Designer: Laura Sowers

Printed in the United States of America, North Mankato, MN.

Table of Contents

All About Sri Lanka

Sri Lanka is an island country in South Asia. It is in the Indian Ocean.

It has two capitals.
They are Colombo and
Sri Jayewardenepura Kotte.

Land and Animals

Mountains rise from the center of Sri Lanka. **Plains** are all around them.

Palm trees grow along beaches. **Lagoons** line the coast.

lagoon

Sri Pada

Size: 7,559 feet (2,304 meters) tall

Famous For: a tall mountain peak that is important to many religions

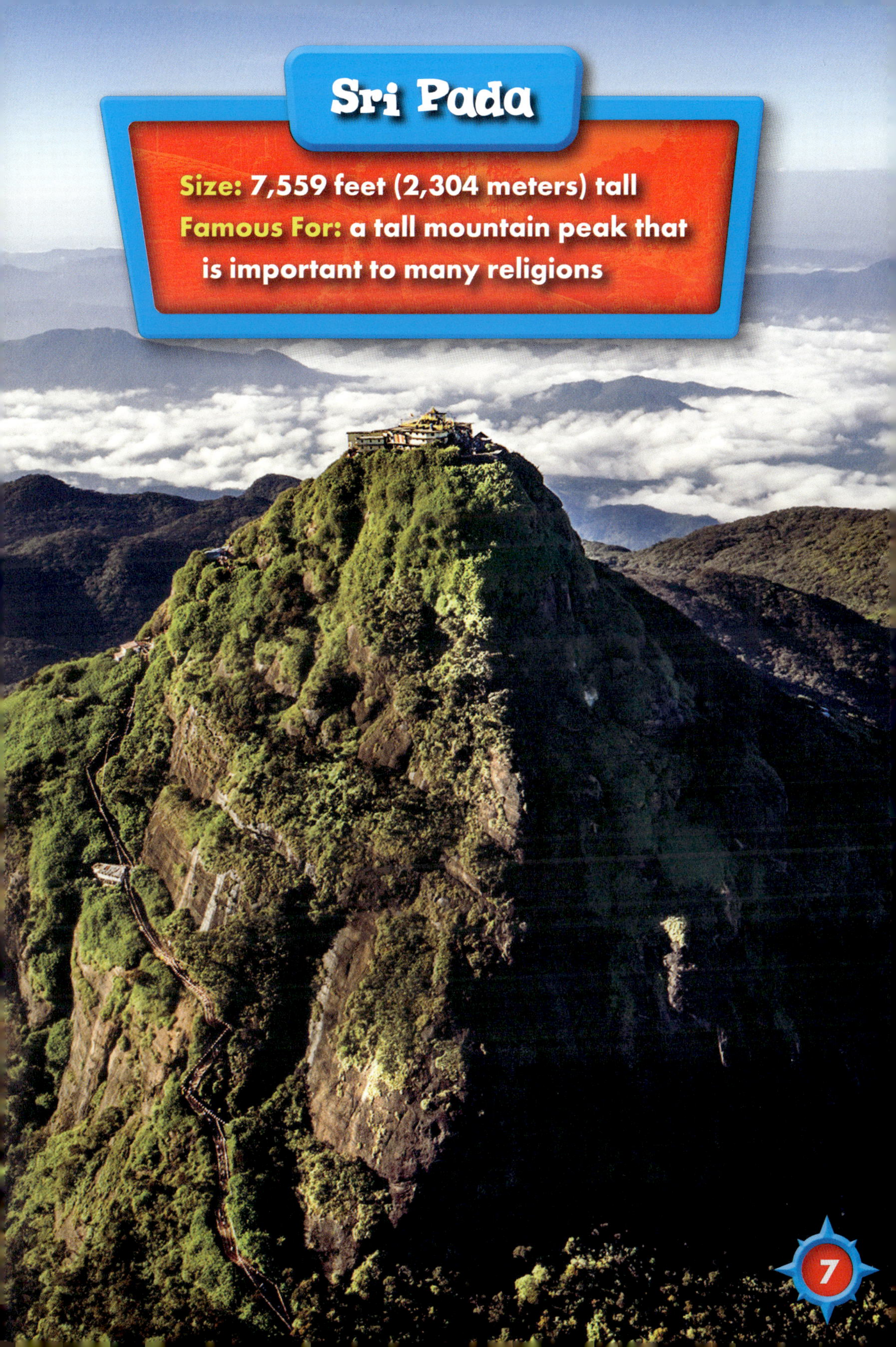

Sri Lanka is **tropical**. The coast is warm. Mountains are cooler.

It rains a lot during **monsoon** seasons. It is dry the rest of the year.

Elephants cool themselves in rivers. Dugongs munch on seagrass along the coast.

Animals of Sri Lanka

Sri Lankan elephant

dugong

leopard

Asian green bee-eater

Leopards chase monkeys in forests at night. Green bee-eaters catch bugs.

Life in Sri Lanka

Most Sri Lankans are Sinhalese. The main language is Sinhala.

Most people live in the country. People practice **Buddhism**.

Buddhist temple

English: Hello
Sinhala: Ayubowan
(eye-yoo-bo-wan)

Volleyball is the national sport. **Cricket** is the most popular sport.

People enjoy music and plays. **Stilt fishing** is common along the southern coast.

stilt fishing

Hot butter cuttlefish is deep-fried. Jackfruit curry is often served with rice.

Sri Lankan Foods

hot butter cuttlefish

jackfruit curry

pol sambol

watalappam

Pol sambol is made with coconut and chiles. *Watalappam* is a coconut dessert.

Every full moon is a holiday. Many Buddhists **fast** and visit **temples**.

The *Esala Perahera* **festival** happens each summer. People watch jugglers and dancers!

Buddhist temple during a full moon

Esala Perahera

Sri Lanka Facts

Size:
25,332 square miles
(65,610 square kilometers)

Population:
21,781,800 (2024)

National Holiday:
National Day (February 4)

Main Languages:
Sinhala, Tamil

Capital Cities:
Colombo and
Sri Jayewardenepura Kotte

Famous Face

Name: Jacqueline Fernandez

Famous For: movie and television actress

Religions

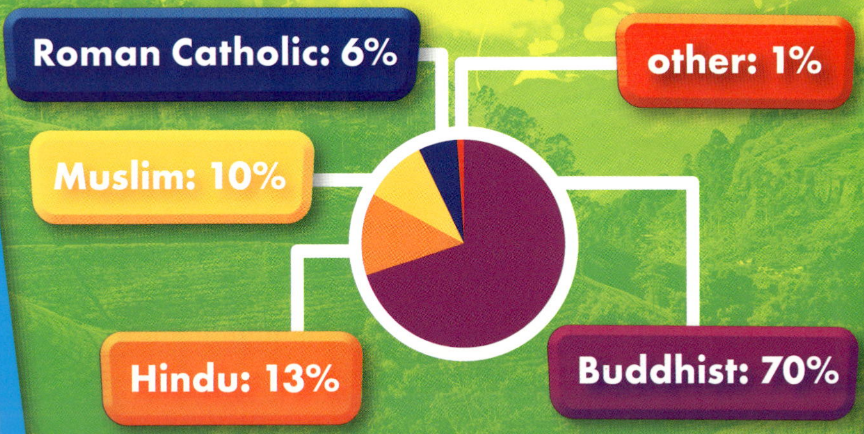

Top Landmarks

Old Town of Galle

Rangiri Dambulla Cave Temple

Sigiriya fortress

Glossary

Buddhism—a religion of eastern and central Asia based on the teachings of Buddha, the founder of Buddhism

cricket—a field game similar to baseball

fast—to go without food or water, often for religious reasons

festival—a time or event of celebration

lagoons—shallow bodies of water blocked from the ocean by coral reefs, atolls, or islands

monsoon—related to winds that change direction each season; monsoons can bring heavy rain.

plains—large areas of flat land

stilt fishing—a type of fishing in which people sit on tall wooden poles to catch fish

temples—places of worship

tropical—having to do with a place that is hot and wet

To Learn More

AT THE LIBRARY

Davies, Monika. *India.* Minneapolis, Minn.: Bellwether Media, 2023.

Ponnambalam, Nimmi, and Siddhartha Padmanabha. *The ABCs of Sri Lanka.* Saint Paul, Minn.: Beaver's Pond Press, 2020.

Shey, Sarah. *Buddhist Festivals and Traditions.* North Mankato, Minn.: Capstone, 2025.

ON THE WEB

FACTSURFER

Factsurfer.com gives you a safe, fun way to find more information.

1. Go to www.factsurfer.com.
2. Enter "Sri Lanka" into the search box and click .
3. Select your book cover to see a list of related content.

Index

The images in this book are reproduced through the courtesy of: Jon Chica, front cover; dudlajzov, front cover, p. 3; Madrugada Verde, pp. 4-5; saiko3p, p. 6; Soloviova Liudmyla, pp. 6-7; ksl, pp. 8-9; Goran, p. 9; Marcel Rudolph-Gajda, pp. 10-11; Ruwan Bambaranda, p. 11 (Sri Lankan elephant); Margarita Hranovska, p. 11 (dugong); Miroslav Srb, p. 11 (leopard); Petr Simon, p. 11 (Asian green bee-eater); MemoryMan, p. 12; SamanWeeratunga, pp. 12-13; Thomas Wyness, p. 14; Sergii Figurnyi, pp. 14-15; srilankan.foodie, p. 16 (hot butter cuttlefish); Mihidum Jayasinghe, p. 16 (jackfruit curry); Paskaran.T, p. 16 (*pol sambol*); uckyo, p. 16 (*watalappam*); imageBROKER.com/ Alamy, pp. 16-17; Dan Lundberg/ Wikipedia, p. 18; Thomas Wyness/ Alamy, pp. 18-19; WH Graphic Design, p. 20 (flag); Flexfxproductions/ Wikipedia, p. 20 (Jacqueline Fernandez); efesenko, p. 21 (Old Town of Galle); Michael Abishek, p. 21 (Rangiri Dambulla Cave Temple); Dmitry, p. 21 (Sigiriya fortress); Sunil Singh, p. 22.